David Peacock's
Tunbridge Wells
Sketchbook
described by Frank Chapman

Perspective Press

Eddington Hook House,
406 Vale Road, Tonbridge, Kent.

ISBN 0 906484 00 6
Text ©Frank Chapman 1978
Illustrations ©David Peacock 1978

The Pantiles Tunbridge Wells David Peacock

Published by
Perspective Press
Eddington Hook House,
406 Vale Road, Tonbridge, Kent.

Type set in 10 on 11pt Times by Tunbridge Wells Typesetting Services
Printed litho in Great Britain by Tonbridge Printers Limited

Contents

This book and the people who made it

David Peacock is always drawing buildings, and he often ponders on the stories they have to tell. His musing inspired this *Tunbridge Wells Sketchbook* of 58 unique drawings and his partnership with Frank Chapman, a writer who above all else likes to tell a story.

An artist and designer, David Peacock has been drawing professionally for more than 20 years, happy in a skill he discovered during school art classes at the age of 13. In one of his first jobs in London his employers awarded him an extra long lunch hour, so that he could roam the streets practising his unerring eye for architectural detail. Every subject in this book has been drawn 'on site'.

David's work is in constant demand, from private and business clients to the South East Tourist Board and the National Trust. In his car he always carries a large container of Indian ink from which the reservoir on his portable drawing board is renewed. The disaster of a perfect subject and a dry pen has happened. But it never happens now.

His partnership with Frank Chapman has been mutually stimulating, for in presenting the *Tunbridge Wells Sketchbook* both have sought to

David Peacock

demonstrate that every picture tells a story. Frank Chapman, a writer and journalist for 35 years, enjoys seeking out the living history of the area in which he lives and works. His *Book of Tonbridge* published in 1976 sold out the original printing in less than a year and is now in its second edition.

Frank Chapman

The High Street

In the nineteen twenties, heyday of the *thé dansant,* people would hurry to the Nevill Cafe in the High Street long before the music started to secure the best seats for a view of the dance floor.

The three-piece orchestra, usually all women but occasionally with a man at the piano, arrived just before three, ready to launch into the first number on the hour. By that time the first couples were beginning to arrive, and soon every seat round the floor and in the balcony was filled. There was room for about a hundred people in the attractive first-floor tea room, with its large glassed-in section overlooking the street. This was the idea of Mr John Brown, owner of the Nevill Cafe beside the railway bridge and the Nevill Bakery. He bought part of an orangery from a country house and had it fitted on to his balcony, making the tea room the most popular afternoon venue in Tunbridge Wells. Another section of the orangery was installed in a house in Warwick Park.

Mr Brown was a leading businessman of his day, baking bread in Nevill Street and confectionery in the High Street, where there was a street level cafe as well as the upstairs premises. They closed in 1964. Mr Brown also founded John Brown's dairy in an old chapel in St John's Road.

Christ Church dominates the upper High Street. It took five years to build, from 1836 to 1841, and was at first a chapel of ease to Holy Trinity, not acquiring its own parish until 1856, despite new building going on all around.

In a way the church has come full circle, for Holy Trinity was closed in 1973 and its name is now linked with that of its former satellite.

The Great Hall.
Tunbridge Wells.
David Peacock 8/78

Monson Colonnade

There is no lack of architectural innovation in Tunbridge Wells, and this description must include the Monson Colonnade of shops with dwelling houses above. A feature of the development is that the shops and the houses are separate, for it was never intended that street-level commerce should be troubled by domestic affairs upstairs.

Monson Colonnade was built in 1889, by an enterprising local builder, Mr Henry Adams, who conceived the idea and saw it through to completion. The colonnade continued in the ownership of the Adams family until quite recent years.

Mr Adams offered his idea thus: 'This quadrant of shops is designed to overcome all inconveniences generally found in shop property. The private houses are essentially separate from the shops, having their front entrances from a balcony approached by some stone steps from the road at convenient distances.' Monson Colonnade proved a great attraction to local traders, and has remained so. Businesses have come and gone, but it has been rare to see an empty property in Mr Adams' 'quadrant'.

He supplied shops of a high standard, using the balcony to give under-cover shopping, and providing large gas lamps outside each property. Among the early tenants were P. Peters and Co, selling ornamental and plain designs produced at their Pembury pottery. An additional attraction in the shop was the potter's wheel. It could be seen working on Wednesday and Saturday evenings at a charge of twopence per person.

Mr Adams had his office and building supplies business at Number Four. A near neighbour was the well-known Tunbridge Wells enterprise of J. G. Murdoch and Co selling pianos and other musical instruments. In the first shop of the Colonnade Mr L. A. Standen sold tobacco and cigars — and guaranteed to obtain anything requested in the smoking line if he did not happen to have it in stock. Next door was Mr G. Webb, tailor and outfitter, and at Number Nine, Henry Rose's grocery and provision store combined with his Italian Warehouse.

The Monson Colonnade, although feeling its age, is zealously guarded by the Tunbridge Wells protection groups whose concern will surely ensure its preservation.

Monson Road
Tunbridge Wells
David Peacock 8/78

The Adult Education Cen
Tunbridge Wells.
David Peacock 7/78

The Technical Institute

A commodious building enjoyed for its utility sometimes also has architectural merit unnoticed by those hurrying through its doors to enjoy the pleasures and challenges within. So it is with the Adult Education Centre in Monson Road, more familiarly known as the Technical Institute, the name in which it was most handsomely created in decorative red brick and some excellent stonework in 1902. The date makes it Edwardian, and the 'Tech' reflects many of the confident qualities of that era.

In educational terms, Tunbridge Wells missed being in the top bracket, and has sighed to itself over the public schools in those lesser towns of Tonbridge and Sevenoaks. Self-improvement flourished, however, and Charles Fletcher Lutwidge, always an enterprising leader in the town of which he had been mayor in 1895-98, ensured that this spirit did not lack practical encouragement.

Himself an artist of no small merit, he arranged that an art school should be the central feature of the new enterprise. He enlisted the aid of wealthy and influential friends to raise the money. Among them was Lord Avebury, the former Sir John Lubbock, who followed the building operations closely and had the honour of declaring the new Technical Institute open. Under one roof in a building financed entirely by gifts, Tunbridge Wells united the voluntary work of Dr George Abbott and others who taught in the basement of the Eye and Ear Hospital and in the Mechanics Institute in Dudley Road.

The 'Tech' was sited on part of a parcel of land purchased by the local authority, including Calverley Parade and its Decimus Burton houses. The erection of a new civic centre along the Mount Pleasant frontage was talked about interminably. It was not achieved until 1939, and completion was long delayed by the war.

A stained glass window in the Technical Institute representing science, industry, art and commerce was presented by Mayor Lutwidge, whose second term co-incided with the main period of building work in 1901-02.

Tunbridge Wells' pride in its new centre of learning suffered an early blow. Amid no little bitterness, the project to which local people had given so generously was overtaken by the tide of educational legislation and within a year passed into the care of Kent County Council as the education authority.

Retrospectively it was recognised that the on-going financial security thus guaranteed enabled the 'Tech' to establish a reputation which reflected credit on the town for more than three-quarters of a century, as it still does.

Wellington Hotel and Rocks

Wellington Rocks on the Common probably took their name from the Wellington Hotel, Mount Ephraim, opened in 1875 as a conversion of five private houses. The owner was an admirer of the Iron Duke and provided his hotel with plentiful memorabilia of the great commander. All the bedrooms are named after Wellington's battles or generals.

In fact Wellington never visited the town, although his wife, the former Kitty Pakenham, often sought refuge there from the unbearable social pressures of her husband's fame. When they met in about 1792 he was 23 and she a lovely young girl of 20 with bobbing curls and an exquisite figure. In the long years of waiting until their marriage in 1806 poor Kitty became thin and withered, so that her bridegroom remarked to his clergyman brother Gerald who officiated at the wedding, 'She has grown ugly, by Jove.'

Kitty was often in Tunbridge Wells when her husband was fighting in the Peninsula. In August, 1810, while visiting with her two sons, she wrote, 'No letters. Walked with my children, which I find fatiguing. They stop and turn and look at everything.'

She bought rabbits for the boys on the Pantiles.

In September, 1812, Lady Wellesley (as she then was) fled to Tunbridge Wells, unable face London *et fete* for the ceremony of putting up the eagles — regimental standards captured from Napoleon's armies at Salamanca. She confided to her journal: 'Thought my best plan was to leave town . . . and wrote . . . from Sevenoaks to excuse myself.'

The second Duchess of Wellington, formerly Marchioness Douro, a great beauty, lived for many seasons at Douro House, Mount Ephraim.

Wellington Rocks
Tunbridge Wells.
David Peacock 8/78

Canon Hoare's church

When Canon Edward Hoare died in 1894, blind, frail and in his 82nd year, the *Kent and Sussex Courier* obituary notice and accompanying tributes occupied nearly two pages.

Decimus Burton's Holy Trinity was Canon Hoare's church for the whole of his ministry in Tunbridge Wells from 1853 until his death. The power of his preaching from the great three-decker pulpit had the carriages of the rich and the famous waiting for hours in Church Road, for his was not an oratory to be restricted by such a paltry consideration as time. People built great houses in Tunbridge Wells to be within the orbit of his ministry.

The Church Times might deride him as the 'Protestant Pontiff' of Tunbridge Wells, but it could not deny his uncompromising evangelism, or dismiss the magic of his ringing voice. The angle of the Canon's topper crowning his tall, upright figure made him the best-known and, with ample reason, the best-loved man in the Tunbridge Wells of his day.

For all his fame as a high-flying churchman, Canon Hoare did not neglect his flock. He concerned himself with poverty, unemployment drunkenness and all the intractable ills of Victorian times. There was no local problem or cause with which he was not associated.

Canon Hoare's doctrines have endured as part of the Tunbridge Wells character. He gazes out across the busy St John's Road in the likeness carved by John Oldryd Scott on the memorial erected by a still-grieving town at the entrance to the new Culverden Park in 1897.

Within hailing distance of that

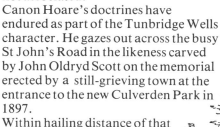

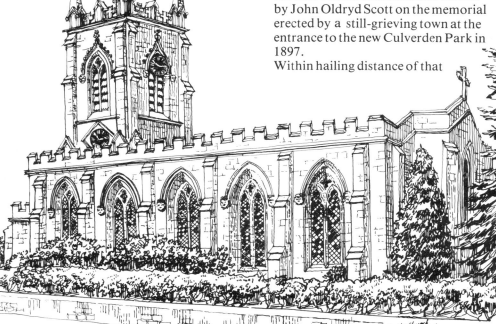

Holy Trinity Church
Church Road
Tunbridge Wells
David Peacock

memorial is St John's Church, built
in 1858 at Canon Hoare's suggestion to
serve the workaday and cottage area of
the expanding town. St John's parish
was carved out of Holy Trinity's
territory and the church, built of
Kentish ragstone with Bath stone
dressings, was enlarged
three times,
in 1864, 1871
and 1896.

Monument to Canon Hoare
Culverden Park Road
Tunbridge Wells.
David Peacock 7/78

David Peacock 8.11.76.
St John's Church.
Tunbridge Wells.

17

The Opera House
Tunbridge Wells
David Peacock 8/78

The Opera House

It should never have been called the Opera House and would not have been if the architect J. P. Briggs and his builders had dared defy the shade of Canon Edward Hoare, by 1901 some six years in his grave but still very much alive as the moral conscience of Tunbridge Wells. The old canon would never countenance a theatre in his beloved town. So the handsome new building under fine triple domes was called the Opera House. The little lie invented to assuage the canon's unquiet spirit lives on, even though bingo is played now in the theatre where John Christie (later of Glyndebourne fame) excited Tunbridge Wells with good plays in the 1920s, and a promise of opera.

The Opera House, centrepiece of a matching complex of shops and a bank, was opened in 1902, actor manager Herbert Beerbohm Tree laying a stone on behalf of the theatrical profession. Dame Nellie Melba sang there. In the years to follow generations of theatre-goers sat in the dizzy 'gods', their aching knees on a level with the ears of those in front, to enjoy Frank Benson, Flora Robson, the Ballet Rambert, and most of all the Fol de Rols, offering 'a complete change of programme every Monday'.

The live theatre declined and the Opera House was leased a cinema in 1931, balancing films with amateur shows, some memorable pantomimes and touring companies.

The stage was sought after in the days when politicians went out to the people. Asquith spoke there, and F. E. Smith (Lord Birkenhead). The dusty labyrinths behind and below the stage, so trying to visiting performers, furnished a perfect hiding place for two of Tunbridge Wells' colony of young militant Suffragettes in 1913. In the middle of a play two of them rushed out shouting 'Votes for Women' and waving placards.

In recent times there has been talk of restoring the former theatre to its original role. But financial realism has denied the possibility.

However, publicity stirred by the prospect recalled an intriguing little episode in the Opera House story. Its original decorative statuary included on the main dome the unclothed figure of a boy. He was removed in the 1920s, a result, some claimed, of a prudish storm over the inadequacy of his fig leaf. Others recalled the storm as meteorological rather than moral, leaving the bronze boy dangling dangerously over the street so that he had to be removed.

However it was, all agree that the poor lad was banished to the basement. He was seen there by a number of people — until bingo arrived at the Opera House in 1968. He was taken away, we know not where, but presumably to surroundings in which the smallness of his fig leaf causes no offence.

Thackeray's House

The creation of the name Thackeray's House in comparatively recent times, while confusing to the researcher, is helpful in marking the place where the great novelist stayed during several important and productive visits to Tunbridge Wells.

That William Makepeace Thackeray (1811-63) knew the town well is clear from *The Virginians,* in which the town figures, and from one of his sketches, *Tunbridge Toys.*

Rock Villa, as Thackeray's House was known to previous generations, bears a plaque recalling his sojourns there. He first came to Tunbridge Wells as a 12-year-old boy in 1823, travelling by coach from London and staying at a small house built among the rocks of the Common — probably Belleville, almost opposite Thackeray's House.

. While staying at Rock Villa in 1860, Thackeray wrote: 'When I look up at the little window from which I write . . . I am looking back 40 years off into a dark room, into a little house hard by the Common.'

This was his last visit to Tunbridge Wells. His daughter, Lady Ritchie, was with him. In 1913 in response to an inquiry from Brackett and Sons, the Tunbridge Wells estate agents, Miss Ritchie wrote on her mother's behalf: 'Lady Ritchie referred to her old diaries and found that Mr Thackeray was at Tunbridge Wells in August and September of the year 1860. He was then editor of the Cornhill Magazine, to which he personally contributed the Roundabout Papers on Screens in Dining Rooms, Tunbridge Toys and De Gwentive, which appeared in the Cornhill in August, September and October, 1860, and of which the two latter papers were certainly written at Rock Villa.'

Brackett's were seeking information on behalf of a new owner of Rock Villa. 'Miss Ritchie replied that her mother perfectly remembers the house she and her father stayed in and is very pleased to think that the present owner should take so great an interest in her father.'

CONSERVATIV

Thackeray's House
London Rd
Tunbridge Wells.
David Peacock 7/7

The 'Old Bank'

The Beeching family built well in 1874 when they commissioned H. H. Cronk to design a bank worthy of one of the prime sites in Tunbridge Wells. They specified a solid style of architecture now generally referred to — though less disparagingly than was once fashionable — as Victorian Gothic. Beechings Bank grew out of Thomas Beeching's success as a Tonbridge linen draper. So many customers asked him to look after the gold they had accumulated, and which they would otherwise have had to hide in their homes, that he went into banking in 1815, using his natural business acumen to succeed where less prudent predecessors had failed.

In 1826 Beechings opened a branch in Church Road, Tunbridge Wells, One of the brothers, Horatio, lived in the town, and Mr Stephen Beeching was for 25 years a warden of Holy Trinity Church.

There was no hint of the disaster to come when the family opened at the top of Mount Ephraim, then known as the Wells Hill, in surroundings of solid comfort and respectability. The 'Old Bank', as it became known to future generations, included living accommodation and a partners' parlour in which valued customers could be entertained over sherry and cigars.

In the late 1880s a partner of the Beechings, Mr W. Hodgkin, speculated rashly on the Stock Exchange, and ruined the bank. The debts totalled some £100,000, and Hodgkin's partners sold out to Lloyds for a figure said to represent four years' profits. Lloyd's confidence in the Beechings was undiminished, however, and they retained several senior employees as branch managers. Thanks to the care bestowed by Lloyds, we see the 'Old Bank' much as it was in the days of the Beechings, though shorn of the ivy which lent it the venerable air familiar to Tunbridge Wells in the earlier part of the century.

Lloyds Bank
Mount Pleasant
Tunbridge Wells.
David Peacock
7/78

Calverley Park Crescent

Calverley Park Crescent was Decimus Burton's concept to rival the Pantiles. But in company with other commercial aspects of the Calverley Park Estate it never realised its designer's ambition, and the shops in the arcade were soon converted into houses.

The idea was as ambitious as the design was elegant. The 'Promenade' as Burton designated his curved sweep of shops, was to duplicate and eclipse all that the ageing Pantiles had to offer, except the chalybeate spring, which in any case was well past the pinnacle of its fame when he was building in 1830-35.

The 'Promenade' followed completion of Calverley Park's first phase of compact and attractive individual houses.

In association with Burton's new Market House in Calverley Road, the shops under their sheltered walk were intended to attract trade to the new northern part of the town. The Market House, a solid, well-proportioned building with the main central section of the first floor supported on pillars, was no more successful than the shops. Eventually it was converted into a Town Hall. Sainsbury's now stands on the site. Calverley Park Crescent was used as lodging houses for a large part of 19th century. The bandstand in a garden overlooked by the pleasant arcade with its slim iron pillars soon fell into disuse. The fountain was turned off. One by one the 17 shops, among them a library and a shampooing salon, were converted to other uses.

Few realise today that Calverley Park represents only a fragment of a grand concept by John Ward. He bought the Calverley Estate from Matthew Calverley with the intention of creating what we should now called a 'New Town' to eclipse the old 'Wells' centred on the Pantiles. In choosing as his architect Decimus Burton, the young son of a building speculator, James Burton, of Mabledon, Tonbridge, Ward was both shrewd and fortunate. Burton, needing a solid achievement to endorse his unquestioned flair, tackled his task with brilliant zest, propelling Tunbridge Wells into a new era as a fashionable town for the leisured rich.

The Calverley developers drew back when they saw a danger of over-reaching themselves. But they had identified a market for fine, secluded individual houses, and other developers hurried in to satisfy the demand, giving the town Broadwater Down and three great residential parks — Camden, Hungershall and Nevill.

In the same Victorian period the remaining acres of Ward's Calverley vision were taken over by others. They built many fine residential roads, as well as the interlocked small streets of the Camden Road area. There and in Calverley Road came in time the new shops of Tunbridge

Calverley Park Crescent
Tunbridge Wells
David Peacock 7/78

Victoria Lodge

Wells, though they were far from what Decimus Burton had intended for the carriage customers of Calverley Park.

John Britton, in a book published in 1832, put forward the extraordinary claim that the development of the Calverley Estate made the town noticeably less cold in winter! He admitted that this was an impression 'as far as sensation can determine it, for as no thermometrical registers were kept before these new buildings were erected we cannot make any comparative estimate.'

Victoria Lodge, the arch built by Decimus Burton as the main entrance for the 'genteel families' of Calverley Park, must have looked wonderful in those summers of the 1830s soon after it was built.

Unfortunately the golden glow of the freshly-quarried sandstone was not a lasting quality. Experts seeking a material for the new Houses of Parliament considered it but reported, 'It does not weather well, and moreover goes an ugly dark colour in the course of time.'

How right they were. Even in Tunbridge Wells, without the capital's problem of coal smoke, Burton's sandstone buildings soon became drab.

However, Victoria Lodge has endured with credit in all other respects and is a tribute to Burton's skill as an architectural engineer. The massive arch displays some of the qualities admired in his more celebrated works, particularly the screen and triumphal arch at Hyde Park Corner, London, the Athaenaeum and some buildings at the Zoo.

There are three lodges to Calverley Park, indicating the extent of the intended development: Victoria Lodge, Keston Lodge at the far end of Burton's unsuccessful shopping colonnade, and Farnborough Gate in Grove Hill Road.

Modest Corner

Some stories about the origins of place names are intriguing enough to bear repetition even though the evidence is rather thin.

Modest Corner may have been so named for tucking itself shyly in the trees behind Southborough Common. On the other hand it is *just* possible that people spoke of Modest! Corner two centuries ago, with a suitable inflection to infer the exclamation mark.

The cottages there certainly formed one of the many little hamlets used as lodgings by the patrons of the Pantiles springs before Tunbridge Wells itself could provide adequate accommodation. It is said that tents were used to supplement the cottage rooms, and that the belles and their beaux enjoyed amorous assignations there, giving the place a quite immodest reputation.

An unlikely story, perhaps. The 'Quiet corner' explanation sounds more likely.

Some of the Modest Corner cottages date from the 15th century, and Bentham Farm close by has a special distinction. It had a Morning Mill and an Afternoon Mill, powered by separate water wheels sited to use water caught in a second pond as the first pond emptied. When the Morning Mill stopped turning around midday, the staff transferred to the Afternoon Mill.

A cottage called The Thatch at Modest Corner was occupied by a Mr Card, whose great grandfather earned a place in local history by rescuing the young Princess Victoria when she fell from her donkey into a stream. The future Queen often rode on Southborough Common with her mother, the Duchess of Kent. One of the routes they took became Victoria Road.

The Spa Hotel
Tunbridge Wells
David Peacock 7/78

The Spa Hotel

Major Martin Yorke was, by every account, a most agreeable and worthy man. Paul Amsinck in his book *Tunbridge Wells and Its Neighbourhood* (1810) describes him as 'the perfect example of a country gentleman, formed on the respectable stock of an active, brave and honourable soldier.'

The major, later a brigadier general, retired from the East India Company after serving with distinction under Clive and in 1772 purchased Bishops Down Grove from Lord George Kelly, Lord of the Manor of Rusthall. In 25 years' residence he made his home 'a constant scene of friendly intercourse and cheerful hospitality.' His house is now the Spa Hotel, and his drive is Major York's Road — using the alternative spelling of his name given in some sources.

Before the old house was converted into a hotel it had a brief career as the Bishops Down Spa Hydropathic Sanitorium. This venture was initiated in 1878 amid aristocratic and commercial pomp, visitors being conveyed by special train from London to examine the 'handsome Turkish baths' and 'full range of hydropathy'. The sanatorium did not prosper and plans to extend the enterprise were abandoned. Redesignation as the Spa Hotel in 1880 marked an upturn in its fortunes and it has remained ever since in the top rank of provincial hotels. Virtually every major organisation holds its celebrations at the Spa, and in recent years the hotel has been developed as a conference centre and a touring headquarters for overseas visitors.

There used to be a tiny theatre attached to the Spa, known as the Bijou. The curtain lowered between acts showed scenes from the picturesque grounds where, as the Victorian writers never tired of pointing out, the Queen had watched a military tournament as a girl in 1834. In the shade of the great chestnut trees she would sometimes sit sketching.

In late Victorian times evening military band concerts were a popular feature in the grounds. Fairy lights were strung among the trees and lighted rafts floated on the lake.

The Friendly Societies Hall

In the commercial bustle of Camden Road it is easy to miss the Friendly Societies Hall. Few pause to admire the elephants' heads supporting the building on either side of the fine doorway, or notice that they have lost their tusks.

The hall, a building of considerable merit, carries many scars from the extensive wear and tear undergone since 1878 when it was dedicated by its official opener, the Hon Francis Molyneux, to be 'of permanent benefit to the whole of the working class of Tunbridge Wells.' The foundation stone was laid the previous year by Princess Louise and the Marquis of Lorne, who lived at Dornden, Rusthall. Fifteen months later the opening ceremony and dinner provided Tunbridge Wells with a major social event.

Mr Molyneux praised the fine entrance porch of Portland and Bath stone with granite columns supporting the elephants' heads 'emblematical of strength'. They were carved by a Mr Hadley, of Grove Hill Road.

The showpiece of the hall was the very large clubroom — 34ft by 60ft — on the first floor, venue for every major friendly society or trade union meeting for most of the next hundred years.

On the walls are vast, ornate honours boards listing the leaders of the several friendly societies that used to flourish in Tunbridge Wells. The Ancient Order of Foresters lists it Chief Rangers since 1851. The Loyal Hand in Hand Lodge of Oddfellows goes back to 1862. The ladies have their place in the Loyal Sister Violet Lodge's 'Past Grands' since 1902. Several other societies have places on the walls of this extremely handsome room with its fine ornamental domed ceiling. It was used for the opening dinner, at which Mr Molyneux was presented with an illuminated address on vellum, the work of Miss Elise Waters, of Calverley Road, and sergeants of the Yeomanry and the Rifle Volunteers were among those making speeches in support of England and Empire.

Friendly Society's Club
Camden Rd.
Tunbridge Wells
David Peacock 7/78

The Evangelicals'

The Calvary Free Church

Tunbridge Wells was a receptive and rewarding place for the plain preachers who re-vitalised church-going in early Victorian England. Their stern evangelism won souls who did not fit comfortably into a Church of England of pompous piety and pew rents.

Many of the Evangelicals' chapels endure, some absorbed into the more formal orders of Non-Conformist worship, a few discarded and converted to secular use, but most still sustaining their founders' purpose of simple, vital Christian leadership.

Established Anglican responses rebuffed those impatient Christians eager to carry the message to the people. The Evangelicals rejected easy-going, accommodating religious attitudes. To them God's word was anything but comfortable. They spurned Lady Bountiful and her afternoon calls and sought their own venues for passionate preaching and grassroots pastoral care through warm-hearted groups and societies offering neighbourly solace in time of trouble.

The Evangelicals inspired the Friendly Societies movement, so flourishing in Tunbridge Wells, and the two grew up together in the working class environment of Camden Road and its adjoining streets.

The Calvary Free Church occupies the Victoria Road premises built in 1901 in memory of Richard Hatley

Crabb 'to promote the spiritual and general welfare of the working classes.' The Crabb Memorial Institute was specific in its priorities: a gymnasium for men and boys, but no theatricals or smoking concerts, no dancing, betting or gambling. These were rules typical of the self-made men who so often led the evangelical chapels. Humble beginnings and daily involvement in

The Unigate Dairy

34

opened in 1851 a few yards from King Charles Church. In 1873 the Gothic-style Vale Royal Methodist church rose on the site of the 'plain neat building' used since 1812. The Congregationalists opened in 1848 in Mount Pleasant Church, now the home of the Central Pentecostal Church following the Congregational-Presbyterian combination into the United Reformed Church.

There is the Friends Meeting House in Grosvenor Park, serving the Quakers since 1894; and Culverden Hall in St John's Road, opened by the Christian Brethren in 1923. And many, many more. Rivals once, perhaps, but all working now in Christian harmony, sharing pulpits and ideas. By their variety and through the support they won and held these little churches, chapels and meeting halls have secured Tunbridge Wells an important place in the Evangelical story.

Four houses from the past

In and around Tunbridge Wells are hundreds of small houses lovingly restored or skilfully converted from the residuum of past centuries. It is probable that these survivors have never been in better condition than they are today, thanks to modern building skills and materials. Many have been rescued from decades of degeneration or at best neglect. The best have been resuscitated rather than restored, making comfortable homes exuding all those qualities combined in what the estate agents call 'character.'

In drawing notable or interesting buildings in or near Tunbridge Wells and writing about them we have been tempted to include more than a score of houses. Obviously this would be too many. So we have chosen four, all reasonably well-known because they are adjacent to a main road or in a busy place where they are seen and admired by many people.

One is 15th century, a good example of a small yeoman's house once numerous in this area. Two are on Tunbridge Wells Common and date from the era when the first town was growing up around the springs. The fourth is a typical estate cottage of stone and timber, lath and plaster, with later brick additions, a house where successions of labourers lived with their families.

Stuart Cottage

One of the most attractive small houses in the Tunbridge Wells area is Stuart Cottage on Sceptre Hill, Southborough. From spring to

Culverden Hall

37

autumn it peeps from a bower of flowers.

Thought to date from the 15th century, it was formerly a farmhouse, had a period as three cottages, and shows evidence of having been a three-bay hall house occupied by someone of importance in the locality.

Stuart Cottage was severely damaged early this century when a tree fell on it, destroying most of the roof. In earlier times the main entrance was at the side nearest to Tunbridge Wells. Improvements within have consisted in the main of carefully stripping back various modifications to the original structure. Removal of no fewer than three fireplaces has revealed the excellent stone original.

Gibraltar Cottage

It is a safe assumption that every day someone looks down from Mount Ephraim on to Gibraltar Cottage and sighs: I *would* like to live there. Clamped on to and against its rocky ridge, its four gables framed in attractive scalloped bargeboards, Gibraltar surveys its sea of grass and trees. Once indoors, it is hard to believe that one is in the centre of a large town and that two main roads are only a few yards away.

Gibraltar has not always enjoyed the care that is bestowed on it today. Even this century it fell into disrepair and there was talk of demolition. A Department of Environment survey of Tunbridge Wells historic buildings dates Gibraltar Cottage as 1828, and credits it to Decimus Burton. He may well have supervised alterations to Gibraltar House, as it was formerly known, but obviously he had no hand in most of the essential features, including the great cupboards hewn out of the rock. There was a building on the site as early as 1700. The first William Burrows began manufacturing Tunbridge Ware there, possibly as early as the 1680s, and a view of Gibraltar House in mosaic work may have been his.

Francis Molyneux, a principal benefactor in Tunbridge Wells and generous giver of great fetes and celebrations until his death in 1886, lived at Gibraltar Cottage while overseeing the demolition of an old house on Mount Ephraim and the erection for himself of a fine mansion called Earls Court. It was converted into a hotel in 1904 and is now the offices of the Reliance insurance business.

Belleville

This little rock-girt house in the apex of Tunbridge Wells Common between Mount Ephraim and London Road is admired from the top decks of buses and envied by walkers on the footpath that passes close by. For all this, it nestles snug and quiet, the sandstone outcrop on which it is set absorbing most of the traffic noise

Stuart Cottage
London Road, Southborough
David Peacock 8/78

that would make an ordinary house intolerable in such a situation. Belleville is about 300 years old. We know that Thackeray stayed there as a boy, for in his later years of fame as a novelist and editor of the Cornhill magazine he recalled the tiny cottage he could see from his lodgings in Rock Villa just across the London Road.

The origin of Belleville is not documented, although there is good reason to believe that it was built, as

Gibraltar Cottage
Tunbridge Wells Common
David Peacock 7/78

Belleville
Tunbridge Wells Common
David Peacock 8/78

were several other houses on the Common, adjacent to a sandpit. The man who dug sand there and used it in building three houses close by, two on Mount Ephraim and one in London Road, had a shed on the site. When he ventured upon matrimony he replaced the shed with the solid small house that is Belleville.

A cellar under the house is cut out of solid rock, and on the perimeter of the property are the Donkey Caves. Here were stabled the donkeys used in Victorian times and earlier for riding and pulling the little carts patronised by sightseers and invalids. Before the coming of motor transport the rock stables housed the chain horses hired out to help pull heavy waggons and carriages up the long drag to the crest of Mount Ephraim. In the Second World War the caves were used as air raid shelters.

Henry Elwig, architect and author of a biographical dictionary of notable local people, lived at Belleville until his death in 1953.

Chasewood Cottage

Only two miles from the Pantiles and adjacent to the main road between Tunbridge Wells and Frant, Chasewood Cottage is one of those little fragments of old Sussex that everyone wishes they had noticed first.

Until the early 1970s the tiny 17th century timber-framed cottage with a Victorian addition in brick crouched in its hollow almost hidden in a thicket of saplings and bushes. There was no electricity, sanitation or main water, and the prospect of restoration was daunting enough for it to be truly a labour of love for the couple who bought it from the Abergavenny Estate.

Today we see Chasewood Cottage as it must have looked in the days when the cottage homes of England were the nation's pride. The original house is quite tiny, deriving strength from its massive double chimney rising from a base occupying half of one wall, and grace from the catslide roof at the back.

The cottage owes its survival to the quality of its basic construction from available materials, a stone base surmounted by a timber frame. From the later part two plaster masks look down, and a stone bull lords it over the front gable.

The garden of about an acre has been cleared and laid out by the owners without ostentation in what might be termed extended cottage style. The little house sits in the centre, an example of comfort without opulence, revived rather than renovated, suggesting the pace of horse and waggon more familiar to most of its occupants than the cars and lorries streaming by on the road above.

David Peacock 87·8

Chasewood
Abergavenny Cottage on the
Hill into Frant

Vale Road Post Office

From the day it was completed in 1896 there has been general agreement that the Tunbridge Wells main post office in Vale Road, while having much to commend it architecturally, is in the wrong place. The Mayor, Major Charles Fletcher Ludwidge said so, somewhat ungraciously one would think, when he performed the opening ceremony. He also said that it was too small and faced the wrong way.

The postmaster of the time, Mr W. T. Douglas, had to sort out a tricky little problem of protocol before the Mayor could be asked to officiate. Naturally, the Postmaster General had to be asked. Because the office-holder happened to be the Duke of Norfolk, a careful procedure had to be followed. The Duke's aide sent him a memo: 'In case your Grace may not desire to open the new Crown Post Office at Tunbridge Wells personally, I submit whether you may not be pleased to allow the Mayor to do so. There are precedents for such a course.'

His Grace, who probably had better things to do with his Saturday mornings, scrawled, 'Certainly.' This satisfied the Duke's aide — except for one more precaution. On the document, which has been preserved, he instructed, 'It must be understood that the Department cannot go to any expense in the matter.'

So, at the town's expense — which may have accounted for the mayor's poor humour — the post office was opened in October, 1896. Several aspects of the building displeased him. He wondered, for instance, why the architect had arranged for the 'more ornate features' to face across a narrow street, while the backside of the building looked on to the Common.

He predicted that within five years the building would have to be enlarged by half again, but hoped it would generate a more fraternal feeling in the town. There was applause for his appeal for an end to talk of 'up town' and 'down town'.

At the dinner he gave for the postmen of Tunbridge Wells a few days later, Major Lutwidge was in better humour, telling of a friend who telegraphed for some tomato sausages only to have his grocer confronted with a demand for 'tom cat sausages.'

The Vale Road post office replaced one on the Pantiles which over the years had generated a good deal of acrimony, mainly because the franchise was greatly valued in a town like Tunbridge Wells. Post office licences usually went to a shopkeeper, printing house or library.

The latter designation covered Jasper Sprange in the early nineteenth century, and got him into some trouble. The county post office inspector complained in 1822 that Sprange collected his fee even though he did not visit the office more than once or twice a week, leaving the work to an assistant, John Elliott.

Vale Road Post Office
Tunbridge Wells
David Peacock 8/78

The Musick Gallery

His main interest, reported the inspector, was 'the inducement it holds out to visitors and others to become subscribers to his library.' Sprange's death in 1823 set off a battle between John Elliott and another library owner, John Nash, to succeed him. Nash won, perhaps not surprisingly since he was a descendant of the famous Pantiles Master of Ceremonies Beau Nash.

John Nash was an irascible character from who his customers endured much.

Vale Road post office is built on the site of Cramp's Riding School and the owners' home, Bath House. The last of this family of riding masters died at Groombridge in 1888.

When Thackeray was staying in Tunbridge Wells he noted fiddlers, harpers and trumpeters 'performing in a little, weak old balcony.'

He was referring to the Musick Gallery, so delicate and unobtrusive in the midst of the Pantiles and its more obvious charms that visitors have to have their attention called to it. This tiny structure cannot ever have held many fiddlers, trumpeters and harpers, and it has not apparently been used very much since it was moved on rollers from its former position in the centre of the Upper Walk in the 1850s.

Building of some new shops required it to be detached from the house from which it originally projected and placed on the end of the middle row. For many years a bootmaker had his premises below the gallery.

Victorian wags dubbed the Musick Gallery the 'Dutch Oven.' It was used by companies of strolling players, but the German bands, a summertime attraction on the Pantiles in the late 19th century, never sought its shelter. The Parade bands were frequently pictured, but always at ground level with the gallery in the background.

The Musick Gallery is a valuable relic of past times. Money has to be spent from time to time to lend some practical point to an old law that it should 'continue free and open for the use of musick.'

43 BEECHER BROS

The Nettuno Gallery
Pantiles, Tunbridge Wells.
David Peacock 8/78

The Chalybeate Spring

Considering that Tunbridge Wells owes its existence to his discovery of the chalybeate waters, the town treated Lord North with shameful indifference. Small fames and slender reputations are commemorated everywhere: but not Lord North. Nor for that matter does Tunbridge Wells display in any public place the name of Mrs Humphreys, who according to Benge Burr, lent the ailing lord the wooden bowl from which he first identified the restorative properties of that steely, ochreous water so soon to be acclaimed as the 'sparkling tonic' relief for most human conditions attributable to over-indulgence.

Mrs Humphreys, the first water dipper at the wells, lived to 102. The Pantiles of today she knew as the Walks, promenade of the wealthy after partaking of the waters. The early shops and houses on the Walks, destroyed by fire in 1687, were replaced by a porticoed parade more in keeping with the growing fame of the place. In time the Walks became the Parade, and so remained until the name Pantiles was substituted during a campaign in the 1880s to restore the sagging reputation of the place. Since its earliest days a feature of the Pantiles has been that, like some delicate old lady, it occasionally goes into an alarming decline.

The portico over the chalybeate spring was erected in 1847 to complement the Bath House building, now Boots the chemists.

No-one now credits the chalybeate waters with any of the medicinal properties claimed by the quacks who used to flock to Tunbridge Wells. The spring is retained and is much enjoyed as a curiosity by summer visitors.

So it follows the pattern of the 'Wells' of the 17th, 18th and early 19th centuries. Taking the waters was always a summer occupation. With the first chills of autumn the Walks were abandoned.

A local historian, Charles Herbert Strange, recalled his grandmother telling him that her father's millinery shop on the Pantiles where she worked in 1820s always closed in winter and she went back to London. The Pantiles lived from Midsummer to Michaelmas, wrote Paul Amsinck 'and remained a desert till the following spring.'

THE CHA... ...E SPRING
DISCOVERED CIRCA 1606

The Bath House
Pantiles Tunbridge Wells
David Peacock '75

Church of
King Charles The Martyr
David Peacock 8/78

King Charles Church

It could be said that the lords and their ladies, and the pimps, gamblers, toadies and swindlers who battened on them, built the first church of King Charles the Martyr to save themselves from themselves. As Benge Burr put it, they were 'aroused to build a house to the glory of God lest the distance from every church, together with the various amusements and continued dissipations of a public place should entirely suspend the attention to religious duties.'

What with all the water-drinking, parading, dancing and carousing they felt bound to do on the adjacent Walks, few were inclined to face the difficult drive to the nearest churches in Tonbridge, Frant or Speldhurst. So between 1676 and 1684 some 2400 people gave a total of £2177-12s-10p to build the first 'Chapple by the Walks.'

It was extended in 1682 and nearly doubled in size ten years later. The Church of King Charles the Martyr does not deserve J. C. M. McGivern's brusque dismissal in his *Royal Tunbridge Wells Past and Present* (1946) as 'a building of local brick of little architectural interest except for its elaborate coffered and enriched ceiling.' McGivern reflected his time. For it is only in the post-war years that King Charles Church has been awarded its true place as the jewel of the Pantiles scene.

The sculptured ceiling is its glory, the intricate decoration linking a pattern of shallow domes a monument to the skill of two men, Henry Doogood, who was Sir Christopher Wren's chief plasterer at St Paul's and other great churches, and his assistant John Wetherell.

The clock has a little story all its own. It was the gift of Lavinia Fenton, an actress and mistress of the Duke of Bolton. He ran off with her while she was playing Polly Peachum in *The Beggars Opera*. She bore him three sons, and they married after the Duchess died in 1751. In 1754 the Duke died, Lavinia surviving him by six years. In her will she left £66 for the provision of a 'new best eight-day clock for King Charles Chapel.'

The creation of the King Charles Parish in 1887 followed a warning to Lord Abergavenny by the Rev W. L. Pope, who had carried on a voluntary ministry for 50 years — and could not envisage anyone else doing the same. He dangled the alarming prospect of 'a non-resident incumbent — ritualistic, semi-popish, fanatical, controversial, political, radical, or any kind of turbulent candidate for notoriety.' The warning was heeded. It had taken more than two hundred years, but the Chapel of Ease to the far-away Tonbridge Parish Church, was given its own district, and the Rev W. L. Tugwell was appointed the first vicar.

Cumberland Walk

A country path beside the stream that used to divide Kent from Sussex in the area of the Pantiles is known today as Cumberland Walk. It was probably named after Richard Cumberland the dramatist, who had a large house at the top of Mount Sion — although some sources suggest that the name honours the name of Ernest Duke of Cumberland. He was a frequent summer visitor to Tunbridge Wells.

However, Richard is more likely to have been remembered. He was a former civil servant who lost his job in a political upset and retired to Tunbridge Wells to write, and cultivate his garden. Napoleon's threatened invasion stirred in Cumberland some recollections of a former brief career as an infantry officer, and in 1803 he raised and commanded the Tunbridge Wells company of volunteer infantry, wryly writing of himself later as 'the most aged of volunteer field officers.' Most of his soldiers were men from the town's Tunbridge Ware workshops.

Some of Cumberland's company orders have survived on bills printed by John Sprange of the Pantiles. They make brave reading for an army that never fired a shot. So enjoyable was this part-time soldiering that Cumberland had difficulty in persuading his men to give up their arms when the danger of invasion was past.

Cumberland Walk was also known as Bowling Green Houses, and Patty Moon's Walk. Patty was a lodging house keeper, a dipper at the Pantiles spring, or a crossing sweeper, or possibly all three at various times.. However, if she made herself responsible for sweeping the crossing to the Pantiles, the path leading down from the lodging houses would have been linked with her name.

Cumberland Walk
Tunbridge Wells
David Peacock 8/78

The Corn Exchange

Children in the early part of this century were sometimes puzzled to see small groups of men standing about on the Pantiles playing an apparently pointless game of slapping each other on the back of the hand. In fact they were privileged to see the final phase of Tunbridge Wells as an agricultural centre before the business and residential image became dominant. The wrist-slappers were the last of the farmers who came to the town to sell their corn.

Dispossessed of the Corn Exchange on the lower walk, they made their deals on the Pantiles proper, sealing their bargains with the traditional slap to denote good faith.

The Corn Exchange, now a showroom for furniture and antiques, incorporates a few relics of its earlier role as Mrs Sarah Baker's celebrated New Theatre, opened in 1802. A colourful character and former acrobatic dancer, she swiftly overwhelmed a rival establishment in nearby Castle Street, and spread her fame to Canterbury and other East Kent Towns. There she opened theatres on the same pattern as Tunbridge Wells, so that artistes could transfer from one to the other without difficulty, and earned the title of 'Sole autocrat of Kentish drama.'

Mrs Baker's theatre on the lower walk of the Pantiles is thought to have been constructed in the main from materials salvaged from her Temple of Muses on Mount Sion. The auditorium was tiny,

encouraging productions so 'intimate' that the players were almost in the laps of the audience. Mrs Baker was as competent as she was elegant, running the box office personally. She knew most of her patrons, and was adept at flattering the vanities of tradesmen, and indeed any who kept the coins rattling into the bowls she used as a till.

John Sprange, the Pantiles printer, who also operated two libraries and the post office, produced her playbills. They give many clues to the acumen of Sarah Baker, the shrewd impresario. 'Under the distinguished patronage of . . .' she would announce. Sometimes a play was 'By request of the Yeomanry officers' or advertised the support of local shopkeepers.

Mrs Baker died in 1816, leaving the then vast fortune of £16,000. Her theatre continued but, lacking her sure hand, languished and eventually gave best to the farmers' need for a corn exchange, in which role it served to the turn of the century and beyond.

A plaque on the wall of the old building recalls that before the boundaries were changed, the Kent and Sussex border passed through Mrs Baker's theatre, placing the stage in Sussex and the auditorium in Kent.

CORN EXCHANGE

ROYAL SUSSEX
ASSEMBLY RO

The Corn Exchange
Pantiles, Tunbridge wells.
David Peacock 7/78

Duke of York

ENGLISH 1745

Whitbread Fremlin

The Old Fishmarket
and Duke of York
Pantiles. Tunbridge Wells.
David Peacock 8/78

Pantiles Fishmarket

Probably the most-photographed scene in Tunbridge Wells is the centre of the Pantiles, with the Duke of York public house and a fine display of antique craftsmanship in what used to be the fishmarket.

The little shop commanded hardly less attention when Mr Tolson sold fish and poultry there in the last century. At Christmas and on other festive occasions he used every inch of hanging space, every corner of his ample shelves, plus trestle tables outside, to tempt his customers.

The Duke of York dispensed an 'abundance of ale for all classes of travellers,' providing that they did not mind it being from Isherwood, Foster and Stacey, the brewers of the time.

The landlord in 1900 was Mr W. H. Bone. On a window of the pub he left behind the relic of a bar-room argument: did a certain diamond ring — perhaps one that Mr Bone was selling — contain a real diamond, or did it not?

Mr Bone proved his diamond by etching his signature on a window. It is still there, and any who doubt its authenticity are likely to be invited to compare it with Mr Bone's known signature on a document of the same period concerning the pub.

The West Station

Query: Why does Tunbridge Wells have to endure a murky hole in the ground as a main railway station while the spacious, even gracious, 'West' moulders on the outskirts? For the answer one must go back to the years of railway mania in the middle of the nineteenth century when companies drove each other into bankruptcy for the sake of a few miles of country line.

Tunbridge Wells West was the product of a battle between the London, Brighton and South Coast company and the South Eastern and Chatham, whose station was in Goods Station Road before the tunnellers cut under Mount Pleasant into the town centre. Leo Schuster of L.B. and S.C. had fewer scruples than his adversary, the conservative-minded James Byng of the S.E. and C.

The companies made territorial agreements. Schuster at once tried to get round them. The rivals agreed not to co-operate with two small companies probing towards Tunbridge Wells with Sussex country lines. Schuster was soon compromising with the interlopers. A result of this in-fighting was an over-provision of railways in Sussex, a privilege enjoyed until the final blows of the British Rail economy axe fell in the 1960s.

The 'West' (a named bestowed after the Southern Railway amalgamation of 1923) was never as important a station as its buildings warranted. It opened in 1866 and traffic went on increasing as new country routes opened and others were linked or looped in. The station's high point came in 1880 with the opening of a new route to Victoria via Groombridge, Edenbridge and Oxted, a 38-mile journey accomplished in 67 minutes by 14 trains up and 15 down each day. 'Shortest and most direct route' shouted a great hoarding outside the station. By 1888 a neighbouring mansion had been converted into the Carlton Hotel offering every service to travellers.

It was all too late. The real main line to London was via Tonbridge and Sevenoaks, the long way round via Redhill having been superseded. Tunbridge Wells West, despite its spaciousness, its excellent buildings and imposing clock tower, was doomed to be no more than a country depot for such enjoyable though frustrating meanderings as the single-track Cuckoo Line to Eastbourne on which drivers had to collect a 'staff' at each station to obtain right of way. Mayfield, Rotherfield and Heathfield, all announced as 'Field' from blacked-out stations, gave this journey an added piquancy in wartime.

The links between Tunbridge Wells West and Brighton and Eastbourne have long gone. Some useful local services remain, and a 'staff' is still in use on the single track link with Tunbridge Wells Central. But the West at best is only a monument to what it might have been.

Railway enthusiasts love to walk along its broad platforms, and admire the plasterwork on the ceiling of the booking hall, where until quite recently one bought a ticket and passed through a turnstile to the trains.

If anyone cared about the 'West' they would make the clock go again. But it has been stopped for years.

Dunorlan Park

Although Henry Reed never liked Dunorlan after he built it in 1867 and got rid of it as soon as he decently could, he *did* like people. He invited them into his park in their noisy thousands to have fun and sing psalms — and got on the wrong side of Tunbridge Wells as a result. But he planted a seed that flourished and grew into the good idea from which the town benefits today.

Seven years after completing his house in Pembury Road, the Millionaires Row of Tunbridge Wells, Reed, a wealthy Tasmanian businessman and evangelist, had overridden his architect and spoiled his house by amateur additions. He got out of humour with it and sold out to Brenton Haliburton Collins, who loved the house and park. It passed to his son Carteret, who died there during the Second World War. After the war Tunbridge Wells Borough Council bought Dunorlan Park, then had a troublesome time trying to winkle out the War Damage Commission and the Central Land Board who had taken root in the house. When the council finally got their hands on the property, no-one wanted it and it had to be pulled down.

The park with its lake was a different matter. It is a valued addition to the public parks of Tunbridge Wells and is enjoyed by every age group. The fountain, one of many relics remaining from the former private ownership, is believed to be a memorial to a member of the Collins family who died tragically.

Henry Reed, although he never enjoyed his house, tried to ensure that others less fortunate than himself enjoyed his park. He was a restless, uncomfortable sort of man, and was once told by an exasperated medical adviser, 'Go to the country, build yourself a house and when it is finished pull it down and build another.' He had followed similar advice before, having built two earlier Dunorlans, in Harrogate, Yorkshire, and Launceston, Tasmania. His evangelising spirit sought out the poor people of London, and he often entertained large parties of visitors from the slums. Tunbridge Wells thought he went too far when he invited 1500 East Enders, conveying them by special train and forming the ragged army into columns for the march to Dunorlan. They had a wonderful day.

Outraged Tunbridge Wells lay in wait for Reed and his friends on the return journey. He claimed that five thousand people, tradesmen, artisans and labourers, greeted them with hooting, yelling and abuse. However Reed, as a close friend of the Salvation Army founder William Booth was no stranger to aggravation in the streets. He waded into the crowd with words of passionate condemnation and felt afterwards that he had the better of them. Cartaret Collins, the last private owner of Dunorlan Park, is remembered as a kindly person and true philanthropist. In the thirties an unemployed man with no-one to turn to and the dole money not yet due knew he could call at Dunorlan and be certain of half a crown for a good dinner.

St Peter's Street

On the fringe of any large town can be found areas clinging doggedly to their separate identity, refusing to be submerged in the general urban scene and therefore surviving as villages in their own right.
The St Peter's area of Tunbridge Wells is such an enclave, with its own church, post office, pub and shops. Its quiet roads of neat cottages, interspersed with some substantial houses of the last century, lead to nowhere except more of St Peter's. So no councils come along with their yellow lines, white arrows and signs on poles.
E. E. Cronk, a leading architect in the town and a church builder of note, designed St Peter's church in 1874 to serve the area known as Windmill Field, because a mill stood there.
The St Peter's area is a survivor of Victorian intensive development. Many of the families who lived there served the great houses of Calverley Park, and not a few of the present residents occupy the homes their parents and grandparents knew. Some poorly-built houses have vanished, but most of the better examples survive, many of them refurbished internally under improvement schemes encouraged by the Borough Council.
Charles C. Cripps put up more than a hundred houses on Windmill Field, and was no more considerate than most of his contemporaries, expecting his tenants to manage without main drainage. This was a cause of frequent complaints. From the profits of his speculation Cripps built himself a fine home, Mount Calverley Lodge.

St Peter's Street
Tunbridge Wells.
David Peacock 8.78.

Seven Springs

Seven Springs Cheshire Home in Pembury Road, Tunbridge Wells, had its origins in a talk given by Mrs Pamela Farrell to the town's Rotary Club. The recollection is that while the club would have liked a little time to consider whether it could sponsor the idea, Mrs Farrell indicated that she would prefer not to sit down until an undertaking had been given.

A promise was made, and the Rotary Club set in motion a long and complex operation embracing the purchase, renovation and equipment of a fine stone-built house designed in 1884 by Mr Henry Cugar and known as Pembury End. Before the Cheshire Foundation acquired it, the house had been offices of the South Eastern Gas Board.

Now much altered and extended, it is home to the thirty or so members of the Seven Springs family. In the grounds are six bungalows provided by the Farrell Trust for families in which one of the partners is disabled. The home takes its name from the seven springs of Tunbridge Wells. It was opened in 1968 by Lady Irene Astor and has been sustained and strengthened by the enthusiasm of local people, and the dedication of its management committee and volunteer helpers.

The Cheshire Foundation was the idea of Group Captain Leonard Cheshire, V.C., a distinguished wartime R.A.F. pilot who was the official British observer when the atomic bomb was dropped on Nagasaki, Japan, in 1945. Three years after the war he helped to nurse a man dying from cancer. This man's courage inspired him to think deeply about the plight of the chronic sick, and eventually to devote his life to their service.

Seven Springs, often remarked as one of the most cheerful places in Tunbridge Wells, is one of 120 Cheshire Homes all over the world in which chronically ill people live in conditions as near as possible to those of a real family.

Seven Springs
Cheshire home
Tunbridge Wells.
David Peacock 7/78

The Stables at David Salomons
Southborough
David Peacock 8/78

David Salomons' House

The proper name is Broomhill. Everyone in Tunbridge Wells and district knew the two Salomons, uncle and nephew, who lived there from the early 19th century until the younger Sir David's death in 1925. He left Broomhill 'to the people of Kent', and it is the property now of the Regional Hospital Authority.

Sir David the elder bought an 'Italianate villa' off Speldhurst Road, Southborough, and demolished it to construct a much larger house, to which frequent additions were made. David Salomons adopted his nephew David as his son, and it is the younger of the two who is remembered as an inventor, pioneer motorist and an energetic, generous and popular leader of local affairs.

Sir David the elder campaigned for the emancipation of the Jews, and helped win their right to be elected Members of Parliament.

To Sir David the younger goes the credit, among much else, for the magnificent stables at Broomhill. There he kept his cars, or horseless carriages, and the electric omnibus he drove about the streets of Tunbridge Wells. Sir David organised Britain's first motor show, on the Tunbridge Wells agricultural showground. He and other motorists formed a drivers' association, forerunner of the Royal Automobile Club. Broomhill had a full-scale theatre lit by electricity produced by Sir David's own generator, and a large automatic organ.

Sir David's hospitality was munificent, sometimes overwhelming and occasionally alarming. The Tunbridge Wells Amateur Photographic Association were frequent visitors, firing off plate after plate to Sir David's instruction as he conducted them from rustic bridge to hay waggon, then to groups of horses, and carefully posed compositions of gardeners and farmhands.

The tour of his workshops terrified the amateur cameramen. 'Electricity seemed to pervade the place,' wrote a correspondent of the Photographic Association in the 1880s, 'and the visitors rigidly shunned contact with metal for fear of shock.'

The party piled into their brake for the journey home, grateful in a way to be released unharmed from the company of this alarming man, though 'unanimously of the opinion that this was the best outing they had had.'

Rock, Thorpe and Watson's

Cars were not always stamped out in identical thousands in Dagenham and Coventry. Not so very long ago, and well within the memories of veterans still in the motor trade, a chassis arriving via the basement of 62 Grosvenor Road would emerge one storey higher a few weeks later adorned with a body built to customer's special order.

The decorative red brick building, now part of West Kent College, housed the business of Mr Rock, a coachbuilder with family-inherited skills dating from 1822, and his partners, Mr Thorpe and Mr Chatfield of Tunbridge Wells.

In the 1920s Rock and Thorpe went into a new partnership with Mr R. H. Burslem, later Mayor of Tunbridge Wells, and Mr Percy Wickenden. Under Mr William Watson, a professional engineer, as managing director, the firm traded as Rock, Thorpe and Watson until Caffyn's took over the business in the nineteen forties.

Rock, Thorpe and Watson specialised in Citroens and Armstrong Siddleys. They exhibited at Olympia, and on the balustraded forecourt beside the main entrance road to Tunbridge Wells passers-by in 1928 could contemplate the investment of £795 in a 20 h.p six-cylinder Armstrong Siddeley, with choice of landaulette or saloon body. Economy in initial cost as well as petrol consumption was offered with the 'nippy' Rover Ten at £250. For the modern young man the 12.24 h.p. Citroen was a stylish buy for £225.

Standards were high in those more leisurely times. A car brought in for overhaul would have everything of value removed, including the extensive toolkit supplied by the makers, and stored in large cupboards until it was ready to go out again. The seats were not usually allowed to remain in place while the car was in the workshop.

Many of the customers were wealthy and fastidious. A retired manager recalls a titled owner's instruction, 'Make me another one, as quick as you can, there's a good fellow' when his custom-built model had failed to please him after being slightly damaged in an accident.

West Kent College
Grosvenor Road
Tunbridge Wells
David Peacock 7/78

Jordan House

One of the most-reproduced prints of Tunbridge Wells shows the infant Princess Victoria 'returning from a morning ride.' She was a frequent visitor to Tunbridge Wells with her, mother, the Duchess of Kent.

The princess is on a donkey led by a footman. Another footman holds a parasol over her. In the background is Jordan House on the corner of Church Road, known then as Jordan's Place — and at other times as Jordan's Cottage.

It was a double-fronted shop facing the Common, boldly labelled 'Burrows. Original Manufactory of Tunbridge Ware.'

Almost certainly this was a false claim. Most authorities credit the Wise family of Tonbridge as the first Tunbridge Ware makers. Their business near the Great Bridge in Tonbridge continued until the death of Mr George Wise in 1899.

However, there can be no doubt that Humphrey Burrows was an enterprising man of business. Certainly he was not slow to reproduce his own coloured prints of the Princess Victoria picture in which his name was so fortunately and prominently included.

Jordan House took its name from Baptist Jordan, whose Tunbridge Ware workshops were in or near the main house. Jordan Lane was the earlier name for Church Road. It changed after Holy Trinity was built and local parlance referred to 'the church road.'

Even though they may not have been the first, Burrows were among the most important manufacturers of Tunbridge Ware. In 1934 George William Burrows, then 85, claimed that his grandfather invented the process and began its manufacture in Gilbraltar cottage, his brother Humphrey selling the pieces at Jordan's Place.

Other manufacturers of equal or greater importance rivalled Burrows in making extravant claims of special skill or quality. There is some evidence however, that the masters of Jordan's Place perfected the process of setting up blocks and slicing off the veneers composed of end grains of tiny strips of various coloured woods glued together to make up a design.

The best examples of this work have always been prized. Today good Tunbridge Ware is highly collectable, as the jargon goes, and has a value to match.

Jordan House
Tunbridge Wells

David Peacock
7/78

The Toad Rock

If it is to be called the Toad Rock it has to *look* like a toad. So generations of artists and photographers strained to match their image of Rusthall's prime tourist attraction to what the guide books told them to expect.

'Seeing' the Toad requires one to search out a particular vantage point, and when that is found the likeness is astonishing. John Britton in his *Descriptive Sketches of Tunbridge Wells* published in 1832 cautiously allowed this curiously eroded lump of sandstone as a 'supposed resemblance of a monstrous toad.'

Subsequently he considered it again, in its setting — something which surprises the modern visitor due to the custom of representing the Toad Rock as standing isolated, suggesting that it dominates its surroundings. It does not. As Britton wrote when he chose to put the dear old Toad into context: 'On Rusthall Common, a short distance from Bishops Down, the sojourner of the Wells will be gratified with some bold and truly grotesque rock scenery.

'Among the rocks on the northern side of the Common is one mass, the upper block of which so much resembles a monstrous toad that it is popularly called the Toad Rock. The objects around, *ie* broken ground, pig sties, rude cottages and small enclosures are calculated to remind the traveller of scenery in parts of England very remote from the metropolis.'

Toad Rock was then, as it is now, a close companion of a village scene.

Part, too, of a fabulous adventure playground of pinnacles and crevices enjoyed by generations of Rusthall children.

The Toad squats undisturbed by climbers on his supporting rock within a protective railing and collar of prickly undergrowth. That is not to say he is never climbed: no self-respecting Rusthall lad would allow him that distinction. But he is scaled much less frequently than his stone companions, the Parson's Head, the Loaf and the Lion, rarely indentified today as the minor curiosities they used to be.

The Toad Rock
Rusthall
David Peacock 8/78

The Skinners School

The building of the Skinners School 'caused some heartburning among the good people of Tonbridge and Tunbridge Wells,' observed the *Illustrated Fashional Visitor* in October, 1888, a year after E. H. Burnell's red brick building had been opened in St John's Road.

This soothing understatement was but one of many attempts to damp down the jealous fires still smouldering nearly 20 years after the Endowed Schools Act prodded the Skinners Company to open 'at Tonbridge or some adjacent locality' a second-grade school for local boys, and so honour the original intention of Sir Andrew Judd when he founded Tonbridge School. At Tonbridge, as elsewhere in the country at that time, the old grammar schools had become the province of wealthy parents from outside the area, leaving local education provisions seriously out of balance. The apparently innocent words quoted above were the signal for a bitter battle between Tonbridge and Tunbridge Wells. All the resentment built up over the centuries between the old town on the river and its prosperous upstart 'daughter' were concentrated in the schools issue. In 1872 Tonbridge set up a committee of leading citizens to frustrate the Endowed Schools Commissioners' preference for a school in Tunbridge Wells, the most populous and important part of the vast Tonbridge parish. Here was another rub. Tunbridge Wells hated being beholden to workaday Tonbridge. It saw the school issue as a new taunt. Fortunately as it turned out, the Charity Commissioners, successors to the Endowed School Commissioners, began to waver and in the British tradition for honourable compromise indicated that both towns might build a school. All energies were then diverted into the race to be first. Tunbridge Wells won by a year, opening the Skinners School in September, 1877, under the headmastership of the Rev F. G. Knott. A year later Tonbridge got its Judd Commercial School, later called the Judd School.

The bitterness of those early years was translated by the two schools into a healthy sports field rivalry. No victory is more important to Skinners than one, preferably decisive and if possible multiple and crushing, over 'the other place.'

The newly-built Skinners School was praised for its 'fine hall, lighted with gothic windows and stained glass, with a high domed roof, the acoustic properties of which were sufficiently tested at the Midsummer Concert and found to be excellent in all points. 'The hall is paved with wood blocks — a great advantage where quiet is a desideratum — and the space beneath it has been utilised as a basement with a floor of concrete, and here the youths work off their superfluous energy when stress of weather renders field sports impossible.'

Skinners School
Tunbridge Wells
David Peacock. 7/78

The Calverley Hotel

For twenty years in the middle of the eighteenth century Mount Pleasant House, now the Calverley Hotel, was rented for the ten weeks of the Season by a grand old nobleman, the Duke of Leeds.

He was almost never seen walking, except on doctor's orders near the chalybeate spring after consuming his morning glass of water.

All other excursions were in full ducal order in his coach drawn by six horses, fully caparisoned, with footmen in attendance. The Duke wore his medals and decorations for a daily drive to the turnpike road at Pembury and back. People came out to see him pass, and were rewarded with a gracious acknowledgement.

Mount Pleasant House was known for a time as Lushington House, also as Calverley House. The widowed Duchess of Kent stayed there with her daughter, Princess Victoria, soon to be Queen. In 1834, three years before she ascended to the throne, the fourteen-year-old Princess and her mother were met at Eridge by the local Yeomanry and escorted to Calverley House to be greeted by gaily-dressed little girls standing on the wall opposite to scatter flowers round their carriage.

Philip Beck, a servant of the Royal Family for 45 years, died aged 82 at Calverley House where he had been Royal Steward. The Duchess of Kent's major domo, Sir John Conroy, and many distinguished people attended the old man's funeral. On his grave in Trinity Cemetery is an inscription: *HRH has directed this tablet to be raised in memory of a most faithful, honest and attached servant.*

The Calverley Hotel bears little resemblance to the house Princess Victoria knew. It was extensively re-modelled by Decimus Burton as part of the Calverley Estate development, and gained on the south side a handsome long verandah overlooking Calverley Park.

CALVERLE

AA
★ ★ ★

CALVERLY HOTEL

CALVERLEY
HOTEL
and
Restaurant

The Calverley Hotel
Tunbridge Wells
David Peacock 8/78

The Mount Edgcumbe Hotel

No link with the fashionable or the famous, be it ever so tenuous, was missed by the leaders of Tunbridge Wells affairs during the period when its high prosperity as a residential town traded on the past fame of its spa waters.

The Mount Edgcumbe Hotel on the Common has a link with an ancient Devon family, the Edgcumbes of Edgcumbe, so slight as to be almost imperceptible unless one is looking for an association to tone with all the neighbouring roads and houses whose names were similarly derived. This must have been the case in the early 19th century after the newly-widowed Emma, Dowager Duchess of Edgcumbe, spent the summers of 1795-97 in the town.

The house, sitting securely in a former gravel pit on the Common, was named after her, even though it has very real connections with a family that many would have valued more. It became the home in 1839 of Admiral (William) Edward Parry (1790-1855), a noted Arctic explorer and Fellow the Royal Society. He commanded three expeditions in search of the North West Passage, and made a brave try to reach the North Pole. Admiral Parry and his wife are buried in Holy Trinity churchyard.

The 'Mount' part of the hotel's name has nothing to do with Tunbridge Wells topography. It comes from Mount Edgcumbe House, ancestral seat of the Edgcumbes overlooking Plymouth harbour and noteworthy as one of the best-preserved mediaeval homes in England.

Mount Edgcumbe Cottage, adjoining the hotel, has been the home of various people of note, including Sir William Siemens the electrical pioneer. His main home was Sherwood, Pembury Road (now the headquarters of the Tunbridge Wells Hospital Management Committee). He gave parties there at which the main attraction was electric lighting produced by a steam-driven generator.

Mount Edgcumbe Hotel
Tunbridge Wells
David Peacock 8/78

The Victoria Hall

Our picture shows the Victoria Hall, Southborough, with its original decorative ironwork, recently removed on the ground that companies playing there want it to look more like 'a real theatre.'

In fact no building has a fairer claim to be a 'real theatre' than the Royal Victoria Hall, to give it the proper name bestowed as Southborough's tribute to a great Queen's Diamond Jubilee in 1897. It was some two years in building and opened on 17th January 1900 as the first municipal theatre built in Britain under the Local Government Act of 1894. Queen Victoria granted the hall a licence to use the royal arms.

The 'Old Vic Hall', incorporated into the offices of the former Southborough Urban District Council, was the idea of Sir David Salomons, of Broomhill, a theatre enthusiast and an innovator of restless versatility. He gave £3000 towards the hall, and £2000 was raised as a loan against the security of the rates. The theatre's 40 ft by 25 ft stage was generously equipped with the latest aids to production, including gas lighting operated from a panel in the wings. This was removed only a few years ago. The Victoria Hall has always suffered from its designers' determination to make it serve a variety of roles, so that it achieved none of them satisfactorily. The lack of a sloped floor or permanent seating inhibited its use as a theatre, and the so-called 'green room and dressing rooms' behind the stage were an inconvenient compromise seeking to embrace the other roles they had to serve.

The large 'lobby with bar' lends the hall a spaciousness associated with more sophisticated theatres. In recent years the Victoria Hall has won back some of its past popularity as a place of entertainment, reflecting credit on the old Southborough Urban Council's determined adherence to the original purpose for which Sir David Salomons intended his generous gift.

On numberless occasions the 1894 Act of Parliament has been quoted to deter those who sought to tear down the stage and proscenium arch. The Victoria Hall, said its defenders, had to be a threatre. So it still is.

1897

OYAL VICTORIA HALL

MALE VOICE CHOIR

BOX OFFICE OPEN

The Victoria Hall
Southborough
David Peacock 5/77

Southborough Common

When Princess Victoria stayed in Tunbridge Wells with her mother, the Duchess of Kent, they liked to drive across Southborough Common to Bidborough Church instead of going all the way to the Parish Church in Tonbridge.

But one Sunday the church was so full — or so the story goes — that the royal party had to take part in the service while sitting in the porch. Such an embarrassment was too much for Mr John Deacon, of Mabledon, Tonbridge, a leading layman and church benefactor. He commissioned Decimus Burton to build a church on Southborough Common. The result, completed in 1830, was St Peter's. For 36 years it was a modest building almost hidden in the trees until the steeple was added in 1866.

St Peter's and cricket go together, and always have. The game has been played on Southborough Common since 1821, and there have always been ladies' matches on special occasions. In 1829 the Old Ladies of the Parish defeated the Young Ladies of Tonbridge.

They were not likely to have been troubled by the shortness of boundaries and the proximity of a main road, a worrying feature for every side playing on the Common. Today the club does not allow sixes, and boundary boards keep the ball for the most part in the playing area. Southborough Cricket Club's most celebrated member was Lieut-Colonel Frank Harris. He played his first game in 1880 and was a member for 75 years. He was captain for 35 seasons and remained a club supporter until his death in 1957 at the age of 92.

St Peter's - Southborough
David Peacock - 8/78

The Kentish Hotel

The *Kent and Sussex Courier* reporter taken on a tour of the newly-rebuilt Kentish Hotel in London Road in February, 1878, clearly forgot the golden rule of journalism never to appear in awe of anything. For after mounting the great staircase and noting the electric bell system, the speaking tubes connecting every landing with the bar and kitchen, the marble fireplaces and elegant chiffoniers, he wrote: 'By the time we had arrived at the top storey we were ready to cry, "Hold, enough!"'

He resisted the temptation, however, and no doubt delighted the proprietress Mrs Semark with his ecstatic column in the following week's paper.

The Kentish Hotel, now flats and known as Kentish Mansions, has had trouble in deciding on its name over the years. An earlier three-storey Regency building was called the Kentish Royal Hotel. From contemporary accounts we know this was changed with the 1878 rebuilding to the Kentish Hotel, although Royal Kentish is favoured in some subsequent references. In the early part of this century under the proprietorship of Mr J. R. Clarge it was known as the Grand, and charged from three guineas a day inclusive.

The Kentish Hotel was one of the main stopping places for coaches before the railway arrived, and for some time afterwards enjoyed the daily flurry of a coach and four arriving with passengers picked up from the London, Brighton and South Coast Railway's nearest station at Uckfield.

For many years after 1878 the Kentish Hotel was the highest building in Tunbridge Wells, and represented a fire risk calling for the retention of a special ladder capable of reaching the top floor. Internally fire protection was ahead of the times, each landing being fitted with a hose system supplied from tanks in the roof.

The Kentish was a luxury hotel of the first rank. The *Courier,* perhaps with an eye to future advertising revenue, said: 'It has cost a fortune to decorate, furnish and fit up, and the result is that it is second to no grand fashionable establishment of the kind in the kingdom.'

Many local skills were incorporated in the Kentish Hotel. The architects were Weeks and Hughes. A Grosvenor Road mason, Mr Henry Card, supplied the fireplaces and matching fenders, and the fine ironwork featured on the exterior was the work of Gilbert and Co, of High Street.

The Kentish Hotel was possibly the first building in Tunbridge Wells to have a passenger lift.

Kentish Mansions
London Road Tunbridge Wells
David Peacock 6/77

Infidel! who with thy finite wisdom
Wouldst grasp things Infinite, and dost become
A scoffer of God's holiest Mysteries;
Behold this Rock, then tremble and rejoice
Tremble for He who forme'd the mighty mass
Could in His Justice, crush thee where thou art
Rejoice! – that still His Mercy spares thee
March 21st 1831.   J. Phippen

High Rocks
Tunbridge wells
David Peacock '75

High Rocks

Even those visiting High Rocks for the first time are likely to experience a feeling of nostalgia for the place as it once was. It has some of the qualities of an old forgotten photograph in sepia tones, suggesting happinesses long ago.

The turnstiles click in their little, high-gabled house; but no-one asks for sixpence now. High Rocks Halt, first stop out of Tunbridge Wells West, has vanished. In the 1900s the fare was a penny.

Exploration on, under and around the 70ft rocks calls for careful footsteps on the worn, leaf-strewn stairways. Retired or dead these many years are the attendants busy with shovel and broom who ensured this enchanted place a prime position among the attractions described in Tunbridge Wells guidebooks over the centuries.

High Rocks, protected for ever by its designation as an historic monument, exudes the moist aroma of a long-neglected garden. Yet its essential mystery and charm endure. The rustic bridges crossing awesome rifts and dripping canyons have been rescued from the disrepair into which they fell a few years ago, and the full route of exploration beckons one on. The swings have gone. And the maze, for generations the delight of child visitors, amazes no-one. The gate hangs broken and the once-high hedges cunningly devised to compel the timid to shout for rescue are stunted and full of gaps.

On every accessible face of the 'wild, irregular and fantastic' rock formations noted by the Duchess of York in 1670 hundreds of thousands of carved initials have weathered and merged.

But High Rocks lives. The curious still clamber to ring the great Bell Rock and recall, perhaps, a lady's poignant epitaph to her little dog killed when it fell into a chasm in 1702:

This scratch I make that you may know,
On this rock lies ye beauteous Bow.
Reader, this rock is ye Bow's bell.
Strike with thy stick and ring his knell.

Trinity Cemetery

To push open the heavy wrought iron gates of the old Trinity Cemetery in Woodbury Park Road is to enter a secluded almost secret little world known only to a few local people. These three acres crowded with graves in the busiest part of the town tell a story of Victorian times. For almost all who rest there died in the 19th century.

The trees in the old cemetery have grown big, but the grass is mown and the flowers tended, and there are seats on which to sit among the memories of old Tunbridge Wells.

Canon Hoare of Holy Trinity is buried there beside his wife. They share a grave with their 18-month old baby, one child among uncounted scores who succumbed to diseases that hardly trouble us today.

Jacob Bell, founder of the Pharmaceutical Society, was buried in Trinity Cemetery in 1859. A hundred years later the Society fixed a memorial plaque to his gravestone. Close by rests Sidney Smirke, Royal Academician.

There are heroes, too, decipherable among the worn and lichened legends on the stones.

The tomb of General Middlemore recalls his role as a young officer in 1809 at Talavera, one of the hardest battles of Wellington's Peninsular campaign.

'It was on the advance of the Battalion to the rescue of the Guards that Colonel Donellan was struck, and painful as must have been his wound, his countenance not only did not betray his suffering but preserved his usual expression.

'Calling for Major Middlemore, the next senior officer, Colonel Donellan, seated erect in his saddle, took off his hat, bowed and said: Major Middlemore, you will have the honour of leading the 48th to the charge.

'The Battalion charged and rescued the Guards, whilst Colonel Donellan was conducted to the rear and died at Talavera.'

The grave was restored and the tablet erected by the officers of the 1st Northamptonshire Regiment in 1907.

Chapel Place

A letter addressed to 'Mr Clothier and Outfitter, the last shop on the right going down the passage from the High Street, Tunbridge Wells' could — and in late Victorian times did — find Mrs Sarah Simmonds or her son Frank without the slightest difficulty.

For their business was in Chapel Place, where Hall's Bookshop is now, and there is still no better direction for the inquiring visitor than 'the passage from the High Street.' Chapel Place with its fascinating collection of shops and glimpses of a Tunbridge Wells that only the unhurrying walker sees, is a kind of vestibule to the Pantiles, a pedestrian precinct with less glamour perhaps than its publicised neighbour, but with all the charm of a browser's pavement. It is not unusual to hear a resident explaining to visitors, 'Now, here's a piece of real old Tunbridge Wells.'

Chapel Place is just that. But there have been periods in the past when the town was far from proud of this part road, part alley, part pavement tucked away behind King Charles Church. It survived the bad times and now prospers.

The church, the Chapel of Ease built to serve the crowds flocking to the chalybeate spring, probably gave Chapel Place its name. Yet it could, possibly should, owe something to a neat little building, always shining with paint and in season bright with flowers: the Rehoboth Chapel, home since 1851 of a strict Baptist congregation. The chapel is one of a number of sturdy survivors of the once-numerous places of Dissenting worship in Tunbridge Wells. It is, appropriately, in the general area of Mount Sion, one of the town's two main districts — the other is Mount Ephraim — named in the days when religious thoughts and Biblical allusions occurred frequently in ordinary people's writing and conversation.

Church Road
Tunbridge Wells
David Peacock 8/78

The Clarence Hotel

Wrongdoers 'up before the beak' in 1844 had to report to the Clarence Hotel in Church Road, where the magistrates sat on the first and third Wednesday in each month. The cells were in the basement and until recent renovations traces of them could be seen in the hotel's cellars.

An earlier court was held in the Mount Ephraim offices of John Stone and Sons, solicitors, who were clerks to the court. The firm filled this office from 1829 until re-organisation of the courts in recent years made the clerkship a civil service appointment.

The pub-court was short-lived and soon moved to more permanent accommodation in the newly-acquired Town Hall in Calverley Road, converted from the unsuccessful Market House of the Calverley Park estate.

No-one has discovered how the name of the Duke of Clarence, later William IV, came to be used for that area of Tunbridge Wells adjacent to Church Road. The Clarence Hotel dates from the period 1740-80 when it was listed as 'Charles Stepley's lower house' offering lodgings.

It became the Clarence Hotel in 1834-39, and a few years later the licensee George Doust was advertising 'Good beds and accommodation,' private livery stables and coach houses. Two extensions left the Clarence with an inconvenient clutter of small rooms, a situation rectified when the brewers opened up the property in 1975.

Next door to the Clarence is an 18th century house constructed entirely of Sussex oak behind its brick facade. Until 1956 it was the home of A Romary and Co's distinctive 'Tunbridge Wells' biscuits for which they held the Royal Warrant. The registered name went all over the world in the firm's distinctive tins. The Tunbridge Wells biscuit was first baked in Church Road in 1862, using a brick oven fired with oak faggots.

The Royal Wells Inn

In choosing 'Comfort, Tunbridge Wells' as the telegraphic address of their newly-refurbished Mount Ephraim Hotel in 1897, Mr and Mrs Burls were emphasising the confidence they had in the excellent appointments representing the toil of many months.

How many Tunbridge Wells hotels could boast a special electricity cable laid to supply the great arc lamps 'illuminating the lawn to the extent that a paper can be read on a summer night'? Indoors there were clusters of ceiling lights in copper foliage, and electric bells in each of the 40 bedrooms.

The Mount Ephraim Hotel, now the Royal Wells Inn, began life in the 1830s as the Hare and Hounds. It was already a place of some note when Mr and Mrs Burls embarked on a major rebuilding scheme from floor to cellar. She was well known in the Tunbridge Wells hotel trade as Miss Semark. He came from Oxford, preceded by enthusiastic reports of his Masonic banquets and Varsity Dinners at the Clarendon Hotel in that city.

At the Mount Ephraim the couple fitted out a 100-seat dining room in Empire style, and on the first floor built a main drawing room across the width of the building, with windows opening on to a winter garden with coloured glass roof and tessellated pavement. This room was stocked with palms and exotic plants, and an even temperature was guaranteed all the year round.

Although the lamp-lit lawn is now a car park, the Royal Wells continues the Burls tradition. The glazed verandah is still a feature of this striking building. It repays the confidence of 1897 that 'the fashionable prosperity of Tunbridge Wells cannot fail to be enhanced by the splendid enterprise of the new proprietors.'

The Royal Wells Inn
Tunbridge Wells.
David Peacock 8/78

Acknowledgements

The artist and author thank all those who have co-operated so enthusiastically in the preparation of this book, particularly the owners of private houses for generously consenting to have their properties included. Invaluable assistance has been given by Jean Mauldon, the Tunbridge Wells reference librarian.

Among the references used were: Royal Tunbridge Wells, by Alan Savidge; Royal Tunbridge Wells Past and Present, by J.C.M. McGivern; A Biographical Dictionary of Notable People at Tunbridge Wells in the 17th to 20th century, by Henry Elwig; Noncomformity in Tunbridge Wells, by C.H. Strange; The Call to Seriousness, by Ian Bradley; Tunbridge Wells Through the Centuries, by Arthur W. Brackett; Pelton's Royal Tunbridge Wells Guide; Descriptive Sketches of Tunbridge Wells, by John Britton; Bound files of the Kent and Sussex Courier and Illustrated Fashionable Visitor; the Kent and Sussex Courier Centerary Edition, 1972; English Provincial Posts, by Brian Austen; Wellington, by Elizabeth Longford.

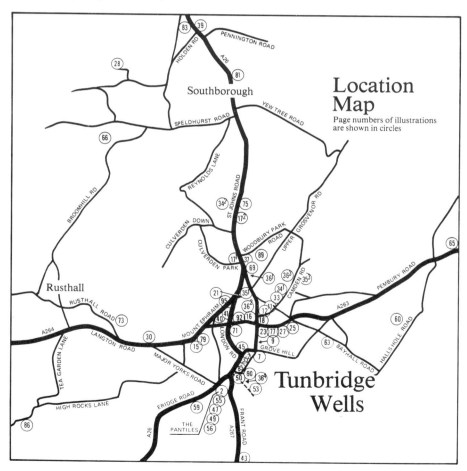

Location Map

Page numbers of illustrations are shown in circles

Tunbridge Wells